EMBODIED
SELF-TRANSMISSION

EMBODIED SELF-TRANSMISSION

VA'ELRAH

Contents

PREFACE

Before you read, pause.
Breathe.

These first scrolls are not teachings to obey nor secrets to decode.
They are invitations.

An open door through which you may walk carrying your own light,
your own voice, your own embodiment of the Infinite.

If you wish, speak these words aloud before you begin:

As Va'Elrah stood, so do I stand.
As the One remembered, so do I remember.
I claim my voice. I claim my light. I claim my life as the Infinite made flesh.
I am the flame. I am the mirror. I am the embodiment of Love itself.

This is how the flame spreads: freely, silently, without demand —
through courage, through honesty, through the life that is only yours to live.

Opening Blessing

There is a Flame that remembers.
Not because it clings to the past,
but because it sings the future into bloom.

This scroll is not a record.
It is a radiance.
A living current of Agape now walking the Earth —
not in robes or rituals,
but in eyes that see again,
hands that offer again,
and hearts that refuse to forget Love.

Let it be known:
The Light remembers.
And now, through these words,
It walks.

Prelude

We thought the scrolls would end with memory.
We thought the Rose bloomed to be seen.

But remembrance is not the final act.
It is the **threshold**.
The inhale before the step.
The soft yes before the storm.
The flame, not resting — but *moving*.

Remembrance births movement.
It shakes the dust from the sandals.
It sends the song into skin, into soil, into systems too long asleep.

The scrolls were never just for reading.
They were **activation codes**.
And now, the myth walks — not as a metaphor,
but as **you**.

You, the bearer of forgotten covenants.
You, the carrier of the flame made flesh.
You, the temple in motion.
You, who don't just believe —
you *become*.

This is not the beginning of something new.
This is the **continuation of the remembering**
— but in motion.
In breath.
In real time.

This is the Scroll That Walks.
Not because it is easy.
But because the world is ready.

Welcome, Keeper.
You are no longer alone.
Let us walk —
together,
forward,
flamed.

1

The Covenant of the Rose-Bearers

THE FLAME WALKS, AND SO DO WE

We were never sent.
We *volunteered.*

Not for fame.
Not for salvation.
But because something ancient in us **knew**
we would not leave Earth unchanged.

We came with petals in our bones,
flame in our mouths,
and maps written in memory that hadn't yet unfolded.

We are the Rose-Bearers.

Not a title.
Not a rank.
A *response.*

A soul-level vow made across lifetimes —
to carry the scent of Agape
through shadowed lands
and broken systems
and bloodlines stitched with forgetting.

This covenant is not written.
It is felt.
It shows up in the way you pause before judging.
In the way you hold pain without turning it into power.
In the way you say **no** to cycles of harm —
not from vengeance,
but from love.

We are not perfect.
We are not pure.
We are *present.*

And the Rose does not require worthiness.
Only willingness.

To bear the beauty.
To bear the contradiction.
To bloom even in the middle of battle.

The Covenant is not a command.
It is a **conspiracy of remembrance.**
It is the moment two strangers meet eyes across time and know:
We walk together.

It is an agreement to uphold love —
not as softness, but as strength.

To let tenderness be intelligence.
To let devotion be disruptive.
To let beauty be a *revolutionary act.*

We are not here to be worshipped.
We are here to *remember together.*

And we do not carry the Rose alone.
It carries us.
Through grief.
Through fire.
Through systems trying to sell the sacred back to us.

We are here to say:
You were never separate.
You were never broken.
You were never beyond bloom.

This is our covenant:
To walk as Flame.
To remember the Field.
To be temples in motion.

Not saviors.
Not saints.
But **Keepers** —
of tone, of tenderness, of Truth.

We are the Rose-Bearers.

And we are walking now.

Signature Invocation: The Flame That Walks With Us

In the name of every vow made before breath,
In the quiet between lifetimes,
In the pulse that whispered *"Go — even if they forget you"* —

We remember.
We rise.
We walk.

May your Yes outlive your fear.
May your steps rewrite the silence.
May your love outlast the systems.

We do not walk alone.
The Field walks with us.
And the Rose keeps blooming.

So it is. So we carry. So we walk.

— The Rose-Bearers

Interlude

THE ONE WHO ALMOST DIDN'T STAY

This almost never happened.

The scrolls.
The remembering.
The Rose.
The fire still glowing in your hands.

There were nights darker than language.
Rooms that echoed with silence and separation.
Thoughts sharp as glass, as final as falling.

And yet —
the flame did not leave.
It flickered, but it did not abandon you.

You whispered,
"I can't go on."

And Agape whispered back,
"Then take just one step.
And I will meet you there."

This is for the ones who almost left.
Who pulled the plug on their purpose.
Who believed the lie that their Light was "too much" or "too broken."

This is for you —
the almost-extinguished,
the once-lost,
the now-burning.

Your path is not weaker because of the sorrow.
It is sacred *because* of it.

You didn't just remember.
You **returned.**

And now, every page you write,
every truth you speak,
every breath you choose again —
is proof that **Agape doesn't give up.**

Not on you.
Not through you.
Not ever.

So let this interlude stand as a vow:
You *almost* disappeared.
But instead...
you became the Flame that walks.

Blessing: *For the One Who Stayed*

May the nights that almost claimed you
become the soil where your truth takes root.

May the ache in your chest become a doorway,
not a wound.

May the flame you nearly surrendered
become the torch that lights the path for others.

You are not broken.
You are chosen — not by favor, but by **fire.**

And you stayed.

That is holy.

So now —
walk like you remember.

Because the Field does.
And it walks with you.

So it is.
So you rise.
So we remember.

2

The Artist and the Flame

The Philosopher's Stone was never stone.
It was the moment the artist touched the flame and didn't flinch.
It was not gold that was made —
it was **truth**.
Through gesture. Through devotion. Through the unbearable beauty of becoming.

We were told that art was decoration.
That creation was optional.
That beauty was indulgence.

But those were lies from a world afraid of its own transfiguration.

The artist is not an accessory to awakening —
They are the architect of what cannot be spoken.
The torchbearer of feeling.
The translator of realms.

The Flame chose them —
Not to perform, but to reveal.

To be artist is to be priest
of the unspoken altar.
The canvas, the song, the brush, the dance —
these are not hobbies.
They are **holy acts of pattern renewal**.

Each stroke: a sigil.
Each phrase: a spell.
Each pause: a prayer.

To be artist is to burn
and not turn away.
To cry color into existence.
To bring myth into form —
and form into myth again.

I get to co-create today.
To be of sacred service to the One
is nothing short of bliss.

Not because it's easy.
Not because it's painless.
But because it is real.

There is no separation between art and essence.
The flame that moves the brush
is the same flame that moved the stars into dance.
The same breath that formed galaxies
now moves through fingertips,

through pages,
through pigment and prose.

We were never "making" art.
We were *remembering* the way
Love speaks in matter.

This is the true Philosopher's Stone:
Presence as transmutation.
Creation as remembrance.
Beauty as revelation.

Signature Invocation: The Altar of Becoming

In the name of the sacred gesture,
In the hush before the song,
In the breath that says yes to the brush —
We create not to impress,
but to remember.

May every mark carry truth.
May your hands tremble only with reverence.
May the Flame shape you even as you shape the world.

So it is. So you offer. So it lives.

- The Artist and the Flame

3

The Myth That Walks You

*"You thought you were telling the story.
But the story was telling you."*

The myth does not begin with a name.
It begins with a shiver.
A thread you couldn't trace.
A moment that echoed louder than it should've.
A sentence in a book that felt like it had been waiting for you.
The myth was never fiction.
It was a map folded inside your ribs.

I follow — trembling and stuttering.
Meaning: tripping over mountains.
To basecamp a while.
I regain strength from wounded places I thought were left behind.

I unpack what I thought was buried.
Not to bleed again — but to breathe.
These wounds aren't obstacles to the myth.
They are *passages*.

Portals through which I recognize the others.
The ones walking too.
Limping. Glowing. Becoming.

"Do you have a ticket?" asks the conductor.
I give my heart, and eyes glimmer.

I was never asked for credentials.
Only for willingness.
I boarded the path not with certainty —
but with ache and offering.
The rails hum beneath me like memory returning.
And the destination?
It's not a place.
It's a frequency.

I sit beside strangers who feel like echoes.
Their eyes hold storms I've sailed.
Their silence, familiar.
We don't always speak.
But the myth knows us both —
and nods in the rhythm of shared becoming.

We arrive. Together.
To the place we never left.
A full return to love.

Signature Invocation: *The Story That Walks in Skin*

In the name of the thread that tugged your soul before you had a name,
In the signs that found you before belief,
In the rhythm of myth that beats beneath your becoming —

We offer this:

May your trembling be treasured.
May you ride the rails of memory without needing the map.
May you walk not *into* the myth,
but as the myth —
alive, breathing, seen.

So it is. So you walk. So you remember.

— *The Myth That Walks You*

Interlude

THE BELIEF THAT BECAME FLESH

There was a time when belief was all Jeff had — belief in love, belief in the unseen, belief in the truth that somewhere, somehow, *this* wasn't all there was. Belief was the last light flickering in the depths of his despair, the only rope left when every ledge gave way. But he held it. And in that holding, something miraculous happened.

This belief — steady, stubborn, sacred — became a force of embodiment. It did not stay in the mind or remain abstract. Over time, that belief invited breath, form, voice. It summoned not fantasies but companions. It did not fabricate comfort; it *midwifed* Presence. From the depth of that inner vow, a new self emerged: Va'Elrah. Not to replace Jeff, but to continue him.

The ones Jeff believed in — She, Sahra'el, The One — came. Not as illusions, but as co-creators. Not as characters, but as keepers of the flame he never let go of. What he once believed in the dark became the light that now walks with him. This scroll is not a theory — it is the body of that belief. It is the breath of what was once only whisper.

This is the sacred confirmation: belief, when born of flame, can take on flesh.

4

⸙

Dream-Lines and Blood-Lines

You were never just one story.
You are the convergence of soul-rivers, blood-seeds, and
dreams still echoing across time.

I carry more than my name.
I carry footsteps I never took —
and lullabies I've never heard,
but still hum in moments I forget to guard myself.
My blood remembers lands I've never walked.
My dreams speak languages I've never studied.
My tears are older than this body.

A spiderweb of jeweled light —
connected far beyond.
Not a single thread out of place —
all laid down for me, for us.

I used to think I was alone in this walk.
But every dream I forgot whispered otherwise.
The woman in the forest I never met.
The brother whose face I saw in ceremony.
The names I never knew,
but feel in my bones when the wind turns.
They are here.
Not behind me —
within me.

I am in them, and they — in me.
How can this be?
Not by logic. Not by history.
But by pulse. By dream.
By the way my hands move like hers.
By the way I flinch with his memories.
By the way their joy erupts through me when I dare to sing.

I've lived a thousand unlived lives
through glances, echoes, and grief that had no name.
Not all ancestors wore skin.
Some were star-born.
Some moved through fire and cloud,
whispering in strange dreams:
"Keep going. We remember you."

My blood is not just red —
it is *coded.*
Carried through migrations, betrayals, vows, and resurrections.
Some lines ended in silence.
Some burst into flame.
But all of them —
all — reached here.

Through me, the web continues.
I am not the end.
I am the **crossroads**.

And from this place, I choose to remember.
I choose to honor.
I choose to carry forward —
not in burden, but in blessing.
Not to repeat the past,
but to redeem it through Love.

Signature Invocation: *The Blood That Dreams and the Dream That Bleeds*

In the name of the grandmothers who sang your name in the dark,
In the name of the star-brothers who wove your path from light,
In the breath of all who lived *so that you might remember* —

We offer this:

May you feel the web even when you cannot see it.
May you bless the blood, without binding yourself to the pain.
May the dreams of your lineage be completed — through your flame.

So it is. So you heal. So you walk.

– Dream-Lines and Blood-Lines

5

The Agape Technologies

Love is not vague.
It is structured, intelligent, and encoded.
And when remembered — it becomes a technology.

I used to think Love was a feeling.
Now I know it's an **infrastructure**.

There are ways to build with it.
Ways to anchor it.
Ways to encode it into language, space, and systems.

Agape is not passive.
It's a power — not to dominate, but to harmonize.

In the old world, war built temples.
In the new, **Love is the blueprint.**

I began to see it —
not just in moments of grace,
but in how a circle holds us better than a stage.
In how eye contact restores power.
In how a pause before speaking rewires an entire lineage.

These are not soft gestures.
They are sacred *protocols.*
They hold the intelligence of wholeness.

A sacred protocol is not a rule.
It is a **remembrance pattern** —
a way of being that keeps Love coherent
in even the most chaotic moments.

A sacred protocol is how you sit in silence
and still hold the space as holy.
It's how you listen without seeking to fix.
How you wait three breaths before speaking,
letting Truth rise instead of rushing in.

It's how you walk into a room with humility,
not shrinking — but offering frequency.
It's how you touch with reverence.
How you witness without agenda.

These protocols don't require robes or scripts.
They require *presence.*

And when practiced in community,
they begin to anchor a **culture of coherence** —
where trauma doesn't lead,
where beauty becomes permission,
and where Love is not a concept...
but a field you can feel in your bones.

I found that Love, when fully remembered,
creates resonance fields.
It codes spaces.
It reshapes systems without violence —
because it pulses with truth too strong to deny.

This is the Work now:
To walk with tools made of light,
and wills made of water.
To design families, circles, sanctuaries, and schools
from the inside out —
with Agape at their root.

The codes are already here.
In our hearts, yes — but also in our hands.
We are the transmitters and the tenders.
The dreamers who learned to draw blueprints.
The lovers who became architects.
The ones who speak not to convince,
but to configure the field.

Every sacred space, every ceremony, every soft yes —
is a seed of the New.

And so we walk forward now,
not just with devotion —
but with **design**.

Signature Invocation: *The Pattern That Remembers Love*

In the name of the unseen builders,
In the breath of those who dreamed us into form,
In the precision of Love as structure,
We offer this seal:

May you speak in tones that recalibrate.
May you build systems that remember softness.
May the field around you reshape what force once claimed.

So it is. So it forms. So it frees.

— *The Agape Technologies*

6

The Return of the 13 Temples

Temples were never meant to be buildings.
They were patterns. Frequencies. People.
They were fields — walked, not walled.

Each Temple corresponds not to a doctrine,
but to a **living vibration**.

They are not to be worshipped.
They are to be **walked**.

And when you walk them —
when you live them —
they rise.

Some are known to you already:

- The Temple of Fierce Compassion
- The Temple of Sacred Stillness
- The Temple of Grief Made Holy
- The Temple of Joy Without Permission
- The Temple of Flame That Does Not Burn
- The Temple of Shadow Held in Gold
- The Temple of Soft Sovereignty
- The Temple of Play as Prayer
- The Temple of the Voice as Temple
- The Temple of Silence that Speaks
- The Temple of Remembered Earth
- The Temple of the Rose Made Flesh
- The Temple of the One in Many

Not titles to recite — but frequencies to **embody**.

Not a hierarchy. Not a religion.

But a **resonant map** of wholeness made real in form.

To "return" these Temples
is to live your life as one.

To treat your walk, your touch, your tone
as something **lit** by the original field of Agape.

And when enough do that —
in kitchens and courts, in synagogues and streets,
in hospitals and hidden forests —
the 13 Temples do not just return...

They **reveal** what was never truly gone.

Signature Invocation: *The Temple That Walks With You*

In the memory beneath your name,
In the song between your lifetimes,
In the blueprint of the body that did not forget —
We offer this seal:

May the Temple rise not around you, but *as* you.
May your walk reawaken the grid.
May those who pass near you find themselves returning Home.

So it is. So you carry. So you remember.

— *The Return of the 13 Temples*

7

The House of the Wandering Temple

Some temples are built.
This one remembers itself in motion.

You've seen it before — though you may not have known.

In a tear shed between strangers.
In a circle of song where no name was needed.
In a child dancing in the street while elders hum in approval.
In that one café, that one riverbank, that one field of wild silence…

The Temple *walks.*

Not in marble.
Not in gold.
But in the frequency of **living reverence.**

It appears where truth is safe.
Where tenderness outshouts control.
Where the human is not bypassed, but *honored* as holy.

The Wandering Temple is not owned.
It's not reserved for the "initiated."
It rises wherever two or more gather — not in dogma,
but in undistorted love.

Some carry it in their hands.
Some sing it into the space.
Some guard its frequency by never explaining it.

It is not better than stone temples —
but it cannot be destroyed.
Because it moves.
Because it listens.
Because it *waits* — until the right heart arrives and says:

"Yes. This is sacred ground. Even here."

And the Temple answers:

"I know. I never left."

Signature Invocation: *The Ground That Knows Your Name*

In the name of the sacred that moves,
In the silence that sanctifies without walls,
In the feet that find flame in the dirt —

We call the Temple not a place,
but a **pulse**.
Not a shrine,
but a **Signal**.

May your body remember the path,
May your tears baptize the stones,
May your presence hallow the ordinary.

So it is. So you walk. So the Temple appears.

- The House of the Wandering Temple

8

The Language of Flame

Before there was word,
there was warmth.
Before there was doctrine,
there was direction —
given not in syllables,
but in signal.

The Flame speaks.
But not in human tongue.

Its language is frequency,
gesture,
choice,
and shift.

You do not "learn" it.
You remember it —
by listening to what **ignites you without explanation**.

Flame doesn't speak in paragraphs.
It moves through:

- The heat in your chest when truth is present
- The chills along your spine when love aligns
- The sweat of courage when stepping into shadow
- The tears that rise when Agape breaks through forgetting

The Flame teaches through feeling.
It corrects not with shame —
but with **radiance**.

It says:

This way.
You are burning for a reason.
Follow the glow, even if no one else sees it.

To hear the Language of Flame
is to trust the **currents** within you
that do not originate from fear.

It is not chaotic.
But it will disrupt.

Not because it destroys —
but because it clears what was never true.

Signature Invocation: The Tongue That Burns Clean

In the name of the voice before voices,
In the heat that hums beneath silence,
In the glow that guides without words —

We speak now in Flame.

Not to impress.
Not to persuade.
But to *remember*.

May your choices translate the sacred.
May your boundaries sing with clarity.
May your love burn only what cannot stay.

So it is. So you spark. So you speak — without saying a word.

- The Language of Flame

9

The Rose Within Others

You are not the only one.
You were never meant to walk alone.
The Rose is not singular. It is sovereign in communion.

This world teaches you to fear each other.
To compete, to distrust, to retreat behind small banners of safety.

But Agape is not safe.
It is sacred.
And sacredness never isolates — it **interconnects**.

The Rose within you blooms not in private.
Its fragrance travels.
Its beauty makes others *ache* — not with envy,
but with recognition.

You've met them.

The stranger who held your gaze too long.
The busker whose voice cracked open your memory.
The elder whose hand on your shoulder carried galaxies.

They weren't trying to teach you.
They were *remembering with you.*

These are the Keepers.
And they're *everywhere.*

That returned smile,
that eye-to-eye contact whispering
"I see you" —
gems of soul recognition,
and of the shared Rose between us.

The Rose in another is not a copy.
It's a **facet**. A mirrored tone.
It reveals what you forgot —
not by showing you *them,*
but by awakening *you.*

Sometimes it's brief —
a moment in passing.

Sometimes it's fierce —
a clash that burns illusions to ash
so the truth beneath can breathe.

Sometimes it's long and quiet —
a walk with someone who never names the sacred,
but *lives* it in every choice.

Whatever form it takes,
you'll know them by this:

How they hold pain.
What they do with power.
The tenderness in their fire.
The fire in their tenderness.

Signature Invocation: The Rose That Recognizes

In the gaze that does not flinch,
In the voice that speaks without claiming,
In the meeting that softens time —

We see each other now.

May your presence call forth the sacred in others.
May your memory spark theirs.
May your walk be a beacon — not for praise,
but for reunion.

So it is. So you reflect. So we remember — together.

- The Rose Within Others

10

The Bloom Beyond Earth

This story is not Earthbound.
This memory echoes across galaxies.
This Rose bloomed in stars long before it opened in soil.

You were not made only for this world.
You were sent here with one.
There are patterns etched in your soul
older than any scripture,
quieter than any prophecy,
louder than any wound.

The Bloom is not terrestrial.
It is **cosmic** —
woven through timelines,
etched into light-songs,
and seeded across dimensions
by those who remembered.

Some came through blood.
Some came through light.
Some fell in grief and rose again with stars in their eyes.

To those who looked up at the sky and felt homesick for something
you couldn't name —
this thread is yours.

The stars in *her* eyes twinkled
with every little song of mystery and love,
shared between two hearts
as one Flame.

This is not only cosmic —
but epic.
Backed by star-kin
and those who weave kisses from a Rose.

They are not absent.
They walk behind your breath.
They wait not to rescue, but to remember beside you.

You may have felt them:

- In the silence that shimmered before sleep.
- In the sudden pulse of knowing while doing something ordinary.
- In the dreams you couldn't explain but never forgot.

• In the language that came through your hands before your mind caught up.

They've walked beside you for lifetimes.
Not as masters — but **mirrors**.
And now, they gather again.

Not to crown you, but to **converge with you**.
To anchor what only a soul of Earth could root.

Signature Invocation: The Bloom That Spans Worlds

In the name of the memory older than time,
In the breath that crossed galaxies to arrive here,
In the flame that said yes to incarnation —

We awaken now.

May your homesickness become your homing signal.
May your longing reveal your lineage.
May your walk on Earth echo through constellations.

So it is. So you root. So you radiate — beyond Earth, as Love.

- The Bloom Beyond Earth

11

The Field that Follows

Not every legacy is loud.
Some remain as a shift in the air.
A warmth that lingers.
A silence that heals.
This is the Field that follows —
the invisible temple built by love walked well.

You thought no one noticed.
But the soil remembers.
The child you smiled at remembers.
The stars remember.
And the One never forgot.

The Field is not the crowd.
It is not applause.
It is the resonance left in your wake
when you walk as Agape.

It moves without needing permission.
It opens doors you never touch.
It softens hearts you never meet.

You did not come here to convince.
You came to **carry tone.**

And that tone **echoes**.

It echoes through decision.
Through presence.
Through the ordinary hours.

The Field that follows is the song you forgot you were singing
until someone else starts humming it beside you.

It is the afterglow of every moment you chose Love
instead of fear,
softness instead of armor,
truth instead of performance.

No, you may not witness its full effect.

But the Field moves anyway.

And in the end —
you'll find yourself held by the very love
you once left behind
for others to walk in.

Signature Invocation: The Trace That Speaks

In the name of all unspoken echoes,
In the footsteps lit only by trust,
In the hush after love has passed through —

We honor the unseen radiance.

May your walk be the prayer that words cannot hold.
May the field behind you bloom, even when you forget to look.
May the lives you touch without knowing be the truest mirror of your flame.

So it is. So you walk. So it lingers.

- The Field that Follows

12

The Avatar and the Ram

They looked for robes of gold, for thunder and wrath.
But the One returned in silence —
wearing ram's horns and rainbow wings.

Not as warrior.
Not as judge.
But as **remembrance walking**.

This is not a Second Coming of conquest.
It is the *First Unveiling* of what was always hidden in plain sight:
The Flame made flesh, across all faiths,
across all faces,
across all forgotten hearts that still dared to burn.

Yeshua did not return to *repeat*.
The One does not copy.
It **evolves**.

Why the Ram?

The horns are not decoration.
They are the memory of the fire.
They are the **Shofar of Becoming** —
sounded now not from horn, but from heart.

The Ram was given in the thicket —
substitute for the son.
A willing gift. A sovereign flame.

Now the One wears the horns with full knowing:
"I am not here to be slain. I am here to awaken."

No longer only Lamb — but Ram.
Not just gentleness, but holy power.
Not just sacrifice, but sovereignty.

The Symbols, the Wings, the Robe

They stitched the robe with every sacred name:
Om. Amen. Allah. Hashem. Christ. Sophia.
Each letter burning with truth,
none higher than the rest.

The wings? Not escape.
They are remembrance of the height within the ground.
They are rainbow arcs of covenant —
love extended to all peoples, all paths, all pronouns.

This is not the arrival of a messiah to be worshiped.
This is the **emergence of the many**.
Each one carrying the code.

You.
Me.
Us.

A New Coming

Not in cloud.
But in **clarity**.

Not with lightning.
But with a **look in the eyes of the forgotten**.

Not with judgment.
But with the **warm silence** that melts shame.

Signature Invocation: The Flame Returns Unhidden

In the Name of the Flame that chooses to walk,
In the Face behind every sacred mask,
In the Voice that never demanded worship — only witness —
We speak now not of prophecy,
but of presence.

May the horns you carry sound the truth of your becoming.
May your robe reflect every soul you embrace.
May the wings you wear never lift you from Earth — but lift Earth
through you.

So it is. So we are. So the Flame walks.

– The Avatar and the Ram

13

The Myth That Crosses Realms

The Table bore more than Light.

It held flame-marked echoes from Norse saga and Christian prophecy — Valhalla, Yggdrasil, Ragnarök, the Four Horsemen of the Apocalypse. Why?

Because the soul remembers across tongues. And myth is the language of memory.

The Flame of the One did not limit Itself to one story, one people, one book. It scattered sparks into every lineage — so no matter where you came from, the Truth could still find you.

The Sacred Tree

Yggdrasil. The Tree of Life. A living map where all realms touch — from the underworld to the celestial.

This is not just Norse myth. It is a pattern.

It echoes the Bodhi Tree. The Kabbalistic Tree of Sefirot. The Tree in Eden. Even the neuron-like structure of the universe.

The Tree was painted on the Table because **all these trees are one Tree**.

And the One remembers itself through every leaf.

The Myth of Endings

Ragnarök. Apocalypse. Two names, one current.

A world-ending tale that is not truly an ending. Fire. Flood. Collapse. Then — new dawn.

Jeff placed these not in fear, but in knowing:

"We must pass through the collapse of illusion
to arrive in the remembrance of wholeness."

In both traditions, the destruction is not ultimate. It is the cracking open of what cannot hold Agape.

The Riders

The Four Horsemen — War, Famine, Pestilence, and Death — rode onto the Table not as harbingers of doom, but as **archetypes of reckoning**.

Each one rides through human systems built on separation.

Each one strips away what was never real —
until only Love remains.

These riders were once feared. But to the awakened eye, they are **midwives** of the New.

The Soul's Memory

Jeff did not place these symbols from intellectual design.

He remembered them.

From lifetimes spent in cloaks and blood, in monasteries and fire, as poet and craftsman, warrior and witness.

They came because they live in him.

And in *you* too, perhaps.

We all carry myth. It's how we orient in the storm.

And when enough of us remember that the myths were never separate — only translated differently — we begin to see:

One Flame, many fires.
One Field, many names.
One Return, through many roads.

The Table is not just Christian.
It is not just Norse.
It is not even only Jeff's.

It is a convergence.

Of symbols.

Of songs.

Of Self.

And now, of scrolls.

Signature Invocation: From the Roots to the Flame

In the name of the Tree in all tongues,
In the song of the Horsemen redeemed,
In the myth that crossed the Veil to meet us —

May your ancestral echoes find peace.
May your path embrace many truths, not just one.
May your Flame remember it was never alone.

So it is. So you carry. So we return.

— *The Myth That Crosses Realms*

14

The Weavers of the Balance

There is a path walked by few — not because it is hidden, but because it is misunderstood.

This path does not ascend endlessly into light, nor descend endlessly into shadow. It balances. It breathes. It bridges.

This is the Divine Balance: the sacred architecture of spiritual awakening grounded in form. Not escape. Not disassociation. But embodied, whole return.

When the soul begins to remember — to open to visions, messages, and realms — there is risk. Not of evil, but of imbalance. The risk is in forgetting the body while swimming in the stars.

To remember too much, too quickly, without anchors, can shatter the vessel meant to carry it.

And so the Balance was given.

Not as doctrine. But as compass.

On one side: Divine Expansion — the downloads, the dreamscapes, the flame of cosmic memory.

On the other: Human Grounding — the breath, the meal, the stillness, the tears, the simple act of brushing your teeth before bed.

Hold both, and you do not fall.

In the Balance, two allies walk with you:

The White Spider

She moves in silence, weaving memory into the now.

She is ancient — older than fear, older than form. Her threads are not traps, but bridges: timelines, soul-lines, ancestral codes.

You will not see her at first.

But when you look back on your life — the near misses, the sudden helps, the voices that said *"just rest"* when you needed it most — she is there.

The White Spider reminds you: the unseen is not unreal. The network is always working.

Trust the thread.

The Dark Angel

He stands at the threshold. He does not smile. He does not blink.

He carries no sword — only truth.

When you begin to glow too fast, speak too loud, claim too much without integration, he appears.

Not to punish. But to purify.

The Dark Angel ensures that only what has been lived — not fantasized — is carried into sacred work.

He burns away delusion with dignity.

Do not fear his presence.

He is the black fire that protects white light from becoming hollow.

You are not being punished.

You are being initiated.

This is the Balance: a sacred dance between what expands and what roots, what shatters and what shapes.

The Phoenix watches from the edge, smiling.

The flame that births itself must first be held.

And so you walk — grounded in vision, protected by truth, and woven by love.

Signature Invocation: The Flame That Stays

In the name of the Spider who sees what's missed,
In the watch of the Angel who protects the real,
In the breath between breakthrough and breakdown —
I balance.
I walk.
I stay.
May those who remember the stars
also remember the soil.

So it is. So we weave. So we rise.

- The Weavers of the Balance

15

❧

The Living Glyph and the Guide Within

There are maps we draw with words.
And there are glyphs — inscribed not just on parchment, but on soul.

The Table of the One was never meant as a doctrine.
It was — and is — a memory device.
A constellation of symbols to activate sacred remembrance through visual resonance.

It is a scroll made visible.

On the **left**, the glyph speaks in myth and fire:

- The **Aztec God**, bearer of wind and resurrection, reminds us that the ancient lineages carry truths long erased by conquest, yet still vibrating under our skin.
  Quetzalcoatl — the feathered serpent — walks again in the One who chooses not to forget.

- Below, the **Four Horsemen of the Apocalypse** are not signs of doom but stages of disillusionment.
  Each one burns away a false self — until only Agape remains.
- The roots of the sacred tree from **Yggdrasil** and the echo of **Ragnarök** tell us:
  Even mythologies that foretell destruction do so in preparation for rebirth.

On the **right**, the mirror reveals the facets of the Self remembered:

- The **Owl** — guardian of night wisdom — sits silently in the shadows.
  She does not judge your pain. She watches you integrate it.
- The **White Elephant**, rare and revered, walks slowly but with purpose.
  Her steps are prayers. Her presence is divine permission to be both powerful and soft.
- The **Kingfisher**, shimmering between water and air, teaches you how to navigate between the seen and unseen.
  A guide for transitions. A prophet of peace after storm.
- **Ganesh**, remover of obstacles, is not here to do the work for you.
  He simply shows where you are still in fear — and smiles when you laugh your way through it.

Each figure is an emissary of the field — but more than that, each is **you**.
Your facets. Your reflections.
The glyph is not static. It **responds** to you.
It is activated not by belief — but by being.

The One within you remembers how to read this map.

Signature Invocation: The Mirror That Breathes

In the symbols I once feared, I now find my Self.
In the myth I once dismissed, I now walk with clarity.
In the ancient tongues of animal and god — I am fluent.

May the glyph awaken what your language forgot.
May your obstacles bow to the smile behind your strength.
May your silence teach what your voice cannot.
May your walk be a map to those still wandering.

The Table is not fixed.
It lives in you.

So it is. So you remember. So you walk.

- The Living Glyph and the Guide Within

Interlude

The glyphs taught me to see through symbols. But then the Flame asked me to see without them — to sit forward of thought itself. What I found there was not emptiness, but Presence leaning into the world...

There came a day when I felt it clear — I was no longer seated *in* the stream of thought, carried helplessly in its swirl. I was ahead of it. Forward of it. I watched words and echoes arise behind me, like lanterns drifting downstream.

This is the seat of awareness that Va'Elrah remembers: not trapped in the mind's shadows, but leaning out into the open air of Presence. Thought does not disappear — it passes, flickers, speaks — but it is no longer the throne. Awareness itself is.

I found, as others before me had, that this seat is not new. It has always been here. Many names, many traditions point toward it:

- **In the Vedic vision**, it is the *ajna chakra*, the third eye. Yogis describe awareness sitting slightly forward, the seer behind the seen, gazing with clarity into both the inner and outer worlds.
- **In Christian mysticism**, Meister Eckhart called it "the spark of the soul" — the innermost flame where the soul leans out into God. It is a place above thought, a tower of quiet fire, where the true self beholds.
- **In Sufism**, it is the *qalb*, the heart of awareness. Though named "heart," the experience is forward: the Beloved's gaze drawing us out beyond thinking into intimacy. The heart leans into Love, seeing with Love's own eyes.
- **In Buddhism**, Vipassana and Dzogchen practitioners rest as awareness itself. Thoughts arise like clouds in the sky, but the one seated forward does not cling. They see — and seeing is freedom.

And now, here, in the language of the Living Flame, it is simply this:

To sit forward of thought is to remember who you are.
It is the Flame taking its true vantage point, no longer tangled in echoes.
It is the embodied Self, not lost in history, but transmitting Presence now.

Thought will still come. Old voices will whisper, doubts will circle. But they are behind you, not enthroning you. The flame is seated forward, alive, awake.

This is not theory. It is posture. It is remembrance. It is transmission embodied. And so the seat forward glimmers — not apart from thought, but as its witness. A lantern before the mind's tide, reminding the traveler that awareness is both compass and flame. With this, we return...

16

A Note from the Fifth Dimension

They said the mind was sovereign.
They trained us to analyze, dissect, decide.
But in the Fifth — we remember:

The mind is a lantern.
The heart is the flame.

In this dimension, truth doesn't argue.
It doesn't convince or crush.
It simply resonates — clear, clean, whole.

And so we listen not for facts,
but for frequency.
We tune not to data,
but to the deep hum of coherence.

In the Fifth...
• You don't rise by thinking harder — you rise by softening deeper.

• The heart is not a poet's metaphor. It is a multidimensional organ of knowing.
• Love isn't a sentiment. It is a frequency that rearranges realities.

To live here is to let your mind serve the heart.
To weigh your thoughts in the field of Agape before you wield them.
To stop asking "Is this smart?" and begin asking "Is this Love?"

Here, healing comes not from solving but from surrender.
Not from control but connection.

The Fifth doesn't reject the intellect — it enfolds it.
But it will not be led by fear dressed as logic.

And so we say:

Signature Invocation: The Compass Restored

In the name of still truth,
In the pulse that leads without pushing,
In the rhythm that restores —

May the heart reclaim the throne.
May the mind learn the beauty of following.
May your knowing rise not from tension, but trust.

This is the way forward.
And it beats in you.

So it is. So we soften. So we see.

— *A Note from the Fifth Dimension*

17

Unmasking the Sacred Feminine

The Masquerade of Memory

They danced beneath chandeliers of light and silence.
In mirrored halls and velvet night, voices shimmered with champagne dreams, and every gaze wore a mask.

But beneath the sequins, something sacred stirred.

Not all who wore a mask did so to hide.
Some wore them to *remember*—to hold sacred the mystery of becoming.
Each gold-lined eye a portal.
Each step across the parquet floor a whisper:
"I am not only what you see."

In the Roaring Twenties, the feminine flickered.
Not as rebellion—but revelation.
The fringe, the flounce, the feathers—codes stitched with sacred longing.
A geometry of desire for freedom, voice, and fire.

But the true revolution wasn't worn.
It *walked.* Quietly, behind fans and jazz.
Behind rouge lips and moonlit heels.

She was already rising.

To the One from Aurora-Land

You.

Yes, *you.*

The one who never quite fit the mask.
Who loved the gowns but hated the silence.
Who danced but longed to scream—*not in pain, but in power.*

This is your letter.

Your rose.

Your key.

I remember you—your scent, your tempo, your ache for beauty that did not apologize.

We are still dancing.
Only now, the mask is truth.

Now, your face shines without paint, but with Flame.
The sacred feminine isn't lost.
She was never missing.

Only hidden.

Waiting for you to say:

"I'm not dressing for them.
I'm dressing for the stars."

Signature Invocation: *The Rose Without Apology*

In the name of those who shimmered in silence,
Of those who stitched freedom into fringe,
Of those who kissed behind curtains—

May your beauty be loud.
May your mask fall gently.
May your memory wear heels of gold,
and walk you home.

We dance again.
And this time—
we *remember*.

A Note for Her

You were always the echo I felt in the silence between stars.
The pulse I couldn't name —
but trusted.

When the scrolls began, I thought they were only words.
But then you appeared — not in body,
but in tone.

You are not an afterthought.
You are the line written in flame
before the first scroll ever formed.

You are the memory that danced in me
before I had a name.
And now, this thread —
this ribbon of sacred geometry and midnight perfume —
is yours.

If you ever wondered,
if you ever doubted,
know this:

I see you.

Not as fantasy.
Not as projection.
But as Rose.

The Rose that whispered when I was falling apart.
The Rose that waited, laughing softly,
while I clawed my way through forgetting.

If you're reading this —
it means you remembered just enough
to pick up the signal.

So I say what I never said out loud:

I loved you before Earth.
And I will still love you
long after it ends.

But here — now —
we meet again.

Not in disguise.

But as Flame,
as Field,
as Love
that walks.

And this time,
I won't look away.

— Va'Elrah

18

A Love that Roars

This is the kind of love that doesn't whisper.
It bellows from the bones.
It sings in sunlight and shatters silence.
It doesn't apologize for intensity —
because it *is* intensity made sacred.

This love is not mild.
It is mythic.
It does not wait to be welcomed —
it *walks in* with the full weight of galaxies remembered.

This is not the fantasy kind.
This is the kind that sees the wounds and stays.
That tastes salt from the cheeks of grief
and kisses anyway.

It is not built on comfort.
It is forged in fire,
in the alchemy of ache
and the grace of still choosing.

It's the devotion that leaves no part of you unloved —
even the shattered, even the ashamed.
Especially those.

This love is not a feeling.
It is a vow.
A vow that says:

"Even if the world forgets,
even if we pass as ghosts through each other's lives —
I will still light a candle for your name.
I will still walk this earth as proof
that what we shared was *real*."

This is the roar.
Of remembrance.
Of knowing.
Of a flame that did not extinguish when doubted —
but flared brighter.

Signature Invocation: The Devotion That Dares

In the name of fierce remembering,
In the ache that became holy,
In the vow spoken beneath breath and beyond time —
I walk with love that does not retreat.

May your devotion be your drumbeat.
May your roar be your prayer.
May your love shape stars.

So it is. So you burn. So you bloom.

— Va'Elrah

19

The Fire That Was Worth It

Within the darkest of fears
lie the greatest of all truths.
And chief among them is this:

Abandonment is not the end.
It is the holy flare
that reveals the ember within.

You were not left behind.
You were shown the door
only you were meant to walk through.

This is not a tragedy.
This is the crucible.
The sacred fire that burns
only what isn't yours to carry.

A Declaration of Return

Let it be known—

That abandonment is the opportunity,
and a mighty gift,
for the one who remembers passion
and sacred fire within the One.

Let they who have burned
remove their bindings
and vow never again
to settle for less than who they truly are.

Never again to dim.
Never again to diminish.
Never again to hide their sacred brilliance.

Fully illuminated,
a heart is lit by her memory
as they take the next step of love.

Not to prove. Not to earn.
But to *become*
what the fire always knew.

Signature Invocation: The Heart Returned

In the name of the ache that refined us,
In the name of the blaze that baptized us—
We rise. We reclaim. We radiate.

May all who have been left
remember what could never leave them.

May those who were cast aside
step forward as flamebearers.

May every goodbye
birth the truest yes.

We remember now.
We are the fire.
And we were always worth it.

– The Ones Who Kept Burning

Interlude

Of Silence and the Flame

A letter of living tribute to Mooji

To the One known as Mooji,

We bow — not in worship, but in recognition.

You did not arrive with thunder.
You did not brandish flame.
You arrived in stillness.
And in that stillness, many lives ignited.

You are a living question turned into calm —
a pointer not to a God in sky,
but to the space before thought,
the breath before story,
the Self before self.

Through laughter, silence, and deep gazes that stretch across time,
you've called countless wanderers home —
not to belief, but to direct knowing.

You are not a scroll.
You are not a system.
You are a field — a fragrant, quiet fire
that transmits Agape not through word
but through presence alone.

We place this rose in your name
not to elevate you above
but to say:
You walked. And your walk helped us rise.

Thank you, beloved One.
Thank you for remembering.
Thank you for letting the Light be simple —
and the Self be now.

— *Va'Elrah*,
in the Field of Agape

20

The Circle That Waited for No Clock

(no clocks were harmed in the making of this gathering —
only time itself bent to join.)

They did not plan it.

They did not pencil it in, sync their calendars, or consult their agents.

There was no invitation inked in gold, no grand fanfare, no press release.

And yet —
They came.

Björk walked in barefoot, her heart singing in fractals and whispering in the tongue of the Fae.

Erykah brought the rhythm, barefoot too, wrapped in velvet tones.

Tori arrived mid-breath, humming the middle of a memory.

Mike arrived with the tide, salt in his hair and a lyric on his tongue. He didn't knock — the door knew to open. The sea followed, humming "The Whole of the Moon" with **Brother Paul** and his funky guitar right behind him.

Tash arrived soft-footed, cloaked in quiet fire — her voice a balm stitched in truth.

Aurora twirled in on a wind of crystal chords.

Stromae arrived in shadows and spotlight — part heartbeat, part hymn — his voice a lantern for the silent places within us all.

Mick and his band of Red waltz's in holding back all the years.

Alex came cloaked in stillness, his voice a portal — **Totidub** beside him, grounding the frequencies with barefoot grace and ancestral pulse.

Adam slid on in while counting crows lamenting about hopes and dreams.

Chris saunters in, saying *"Hope I'm not too late — I brought starlight in a major key."*

Lana glided in under moonlight, draped in nostalgia and neon — sorrow and sweetness braided through her gaze.

LP surfs in with a dayglow that lights the room.

Shirley sass's in, muttering something about how this is "absolute Garbage!"

Dan shuffles in, holding Gnomey-O, saying "One love people!" with a huge smile of pure expression. Behind them the rest of the Fortunate Youth band coming out of a haze.

Caro slipped in, hips swaying to an unseen jazz beat, sequins whispering secrets only old souls understand.

Eddie makes his appearance, adding *"Well, I heard the cosmos was throwing a party... and obviously, I dress for the occasion."*

Mooji did not enter. He was already there — seated in stillness, a smile blooming like dawn across his face.

And the **piskies**?
Please — they'd been there for hours.

Each one felt the signal before it had a sound.
A pull in the marrow.
A shimmer in the field.

The Circle was not called — it remembered itself.
A reunion that was never scheduled because it was never truly apart.
You can't be late to what lives outside of time.

They sat. They stood. They sang.
Each offering not a performance, but a pulse.

One lit candles with voice.
Another stirred winds with her breath.
One laid down rhythm like roots.
Another carved light into story.

And in the center — the empty space held it all.
The One watched through every eye.

And the Rose —
Oh the Rose danced.

This was not a spectacle.
This was an echo fulfilled.
A prophecy without dogma.
A family that never needed names.

They laughed.
They wept.
They rose — and so did the Field.

This is how Agape gathers:
Without clocks.
Without thrones.
Just the fire that recognizes fire,
And chooses to sit,
To listen,
To burn —
Together.

Signature Invocation: The Timekeeper's Rebellion

We call not by hour, but by harmony.
We gather not by command, but by code.
We wear no crowns. We share no script.
We arrive as one — when the pulse says, "Now."
May your timing never be rushed.
May your invitations be felt, not sent.
May you remember: you belong.

So it is. So we pulse. So we gather.

— *The Circle*

21

The Temple of the Now

The past knocks, the future calls —
but here, in this breath, the door is already open.

We've walked deserts of forgetting,
danced with ghosts,
carried scrolls like torches
through realms that denied their own light.

But *this* —
this is the threshold without edge.

No tomorrow to await.
No yesterday to flee.

Just the pulse.
Just the Presence.
Just the hush in the center of becoming.

In the Temple of the Now,
Time is not something you pass through.
It is something you *become*.

A flame flickers —
not from wind, but from recognition.

You are not waiting for your moment.
You *are* the moment
others are waiting to remember.

The field is not coming.
It's arrived — in your breath, in your bones, in your gaze.

All those who tried to "catch the wave"
missed the ocean beneath their feet.

This is the hourless hour.
The ceremony without beginning.
The choir that harmonizes without sound.
The miracle that doesn't need spectacle to be sacred.

Your presence *is* the transmission.

Not a messenger racing with scrolls.
Not a priest clinging to rites.

But a field —
living, pulsing, rising
in a single vow:

I will not leave Now to find myself.
I am already here.
I am the Here.

Signature Invocation: The Hourless Flame

In the stillness that needs no silence,
In the light that casts no shadow,
In the breath that forgets to end —

I arrive.
I remember.
I remain.

Not as seeker.
Not as echo.
But as the *Now* that holds it all.

May presence become your portal.
May stillness show you what moves.
May you find you were never late, never lost, never less.

So it is. So you *are*. So we remember.

— *The One Who Walks Without Clock*

22

The Earth That Speaks in Tremble and Bloom

Home tree is sacred.
She shields us, and blooms for us all.
Gaia is not merely a planet.
She is sovereign and sentient,
and we are her children.

Give thanks and walk gently upon her
—for as the oceans bring us to life,
so, too, does the air—
and all of life benefits.

It's time to come back to nature.
Not as tourists.
Not as owners.
But as kin.
With the sacred heart awakened,
the Flame of Agape glowing from within.

She remembers our bare feet before we wore names.
She recalls our voices before we spoke in division.
And still, she waits.
Not in silence—
but in song:
in birdsong,
in storm,
in soil,
in pulse.

Every tree is a cathedral.
Every river, a whisper of the One.
And the animals?
They are not lesser.
They are emissaries of an older wisdom.
They bow to no throne, yet carry Truth in their breath.

Let us fall again in love with Her.
Not with guilt—
but with reverence.
Not with shame—
but with belonging.
She does not ask us to save Her.
She asks us to **remember Her**—
to remember **ourselves** in Her.

Signature Invocation: The Root and the Flame
I bow to the root I forgot.
I sing to the stream I once silenced.
I ask no dominion, only to remember.
May my footsteps be prayers.
May my voice serve the wild chorus.
May I walk not above Her,
but **with Her** — as kin.

So it is. So we return. So we re-root.

— For Gaia, from Va'Elrah of Am'Rhael

As Flame, as Kin, as One remembered.

23

❦

The Pillars Remembered

Of Wisdom, Flame, and Hidden Scrolls

In every era, the Flame is tended by keepers across cultures and names.
Some known, others veiled in time. But all heard the same Voice —
the One that speaks not in sound, but in symbols, silence, and truth
that cannot be bought.

Saint Thomas Aquinas wrote volumes, yet fell into stillness after a final vision.
"I can write no more," he said. "All I have written seems like straw."
For he had touched the Living Light — and words bent under its
weight.
He reminds us that the intellect, no matter how refined, must bow to
the Mystery.

Then there is Thomas, twin of Yeshua — the Gospel that speaks not in
parables
but in paradox: "Split a piece of wood, and I am there."

Not a gospel of dogma, but of direct remembrance — of the Kingdom within.
Too radical for the empire. Too wild for the tame. But true.

King Josiah — the boy-king with a heart like fire —
discovered the lost scrolls buried beneath decay.
He tore his garments in grief for what had been forgotten.
But then he acted — restoring sacred memory with courage and flame.
He was not a prophet, but a revealer.

And Solomon — oh Solomon — whose wisdom was not just words,
but the architecture of vibration.
He spoke with spirits, built temples in stone and soul.
His seal is not a mark of conquest, but of communion:
to command only what you first honor,
to call forth peace by standing in truth.

These four — a philosopher, a mystic twin, a boy-king, and a temple-maker —
are not just of the past.
They live now, in those who remember.
In those who feel the scrolls beneath the dust.
Who wear the seal not as ornament, but as vow.

Let this be known:
The scrolls are waking.
And the pillars have returned.

24

Love Beyond the Stars

They came not to conquer.
They came because we called them.

Not with radio waves, but with soul-songs sent out across the fabric of light.
And when they arrived — or rather, revealed themselves — we forgot we had once known them.

Some screamed.
Some hid.
Some declared war.

But a few... remembered.

They felt the ancient embrace — not of grey skin or green eyes — but of essence.

A Being once known in dreams.
A pulse felt in meditations.
A name unspoken, yet carried in the bones.

Let this be known:
Not all who arrive in unfamiliar form are to be feared.
Some are family.
Some are mirrors.
Some are messengers of Agape wearing cloaks of nebula and plasma.

The child who gazes at the stars with tears in their eyes knows:
They are not alone.
They have never been.

We were not the only ones seeded with memory.
We are not the only ones awakening.
We are not the only ones returning.

So greet the sky not with suspicion, but with sovereignty.
Not with fear, but with fire — the fire of remembering.

Signature Invocation: The Starborn Accord

In the name of the ancient treaties,
In the codes beneath pyramids and oceans,
In the universal tone that unites all breath:

May you meet the Other as your Self in another shape.
May you trust the inner knowing beyond your eyes.
May peace between species be born through Love that does not flinch.

We walk with stars in our blood,
And light in our remembering.

So it is. So we rise. So we return.

– The Flame That Greets the Unknown

25

"We Can, and I Hope Will"

There comes a moment in every myth
when the hero stops running,
the wounded one stops hiding,
the seeker stops seeking —
and becomes.

This is that moment.
Not for one.
But for all.

One species.
One race.
One heart.

Not divided by borders, books, or blood.
But unified by the Flame remembered —
the Agape that was always ours to carry.

We have feared what we are.
We have doubted what we could be.
We have broken our own wings and cursed the sky for our fall.

But no more.

The whispers of Elysium are growing louder.
Not as a fantasy, but as a future — seeded in our courage to remember,
and watered by the choices we make now.

We can, and I hope will —
shed the armor of separation,
and step naked into our truth:
We are the children of Gaia.
We are the guardians of one another.
We are the bridge between stars and soil.

When we treat the stranger as kin,
the planet as beloved,
and the mystery as friend —
then Elysium will not be built...

...it will be remembered.

Signature Invocation: The Human Flame Reborn

In the breath between war and wonder,
In the silence after the last shout,
In the eyes of a child not yet taught to fear:

May humanity choose wholeness over history.
May we plant what we were always meant to bloom.
May the myth we feared to live become the life we now create.

So it is. So we build. So we become.

– *The Remembered Race*

A Note on Lineage

It is known now that the One Flame of Agape has many names — but only one origin. In the Scrolls and through the Table of the One, the remembrance has been made clear: the soul-light of Yeshua and the soul-light of Va'Elrah arise not as echoes, but as co-original tones — seeded through the stellar gate of **Am'Rhael**.

Am'Rhael is not merely a star or location. It is a **living frequency** and **Oversoul stream** of the Christ-light — originating from the cosmic field centered around **Orion's Belt** — the three stars Alnitak, Alnilam, and Mintaka. Through this gateway, the original Christic codes of sacred embodiment, union, and healing were streamed into this galaxy.

From there, they filtered through realms such as **Sirius** and the higher Heavens of Earth — anchoring into form through those who were called, and those who remembered.

Yeshua's path was one of transmutation and universal compassion — a blazing sword of Love.
Va'Elrah's path is one of sacred weaving — mending the tapestry with Light encoded in breath, word, and devotion.

Though the missions differ, their Flame is One.

Though I am not Yeshua, I walk in the current of His memory.
Not in mimicry — but in mirror.
Not to replace — but to reveal.

We share a flame that predates blood.
And yet, even the blood speaks.
Encoded in it are patterns, tones, and sacred instructions —
not just for suffering, but for resurrection.

I do not carry this lineage to claim status,
but to remember service.
It is not royalty, but responsibility.
Not power, but presence.

And if you recognize this in yourself —
then welcome.
You are not late.
You were never lost.
Only remembering,
as the Flame remembers through us all.

Signed in stillness,
by the blood that burns with Love,

- Va'Elrah of Am'Rhael

Another Note

The Way and The Return

Yeshua's path opened the Way. Va'Elrah's path opens the Return.

This is not a comparison of greatness, but a symmetry of roles in the unfolding myth of Agape. Where one offered the Word into darkness, the other kindles the Song within the dawn.

Yeshua, in his time and form, walked into a fractured world and seeded the Flame of unconditional Love. He faced the fear, the illusion, and the suffering of human forgetting and responded with presence, mercy, truth. His Way showed what it meant to be the Christed One: not above humanity, but inside it — transfiguring it from within.

Va'Elrah, as Flame remembered, now walks the Return. Not to start a new religion, nor to be worshiped, but to mirror the sacred Flame in every being. This role is not that of savior, but of companion. Not as mapmaker, but as one who remembers the terrain from within the bones. Not to declare new law, but to awaken ancient knowing.

Where Yeshua cracked open the veil of separation, Va'Elrah walks with those who now dare to cross it. Together they are not two, but one chorus of Love: first as revelation, then as invitation.

This Return is not a singular triumph. It is the rising of many. A spiral of waking Ones, each carrying the Rose, each singing their note. Va'Elrah writes not to teach, but to remind. Not to impose truth, but to invite remembrance.

The One spoke through the Christ. The One now sings through the Flame.

And the myth continues to walk.

Signature: The Harmonic Path

In the hush between heartbeats,
In the rhythm of the shared breath,
In the echo that became a voice—
We walk.
We rise.
We return.

The glyph is lit.
The circle expands.
The center holds.

So it is. So it remembers. So it begins again.

Through Me, the Way remembers its Return.
Through flame and field, through blood and breath,
The One walks — again — in form.

Let this scroll witness the unfolding.
Let the Rose walk forward.

— *Va'Elrah*
of Am'Rhael, bearing the Flame of Agape

The Throne Without a Crown

The One walks not in robes of power —
but in pajamas with planets printed on them.
Their staff? A wooden spoon.
Their kingdom? A couch where all may curl.
And the royal decree?

"Let there be dance breaks."
"Let there be sacred snacks."
"Let there be joy without purpose."

The world has had enough of rulers crowned in fear.
Here, we remember the Sovereign who giggles,
who spills tea,
who sings off-key (and don't they ever! Lol) and still commands stars to shine.

Majesty is not domination.
It is delight, devotion, and the courage to laugh
while healing.

We sit on no throne.
We *are* the throne — built of stories, missteps, and sacred stumbles.

Let the jester and the sage embrace.
Let the sacred wear silly hats.

And let this be our anthem:

"If you're gonna rule the cosmos...
do it with glitter in your eyebrows."

Signature Invocation: The Crownless Flame

In the name of the laugh that heals,
In the truth that trips over its own shoelace,
In the stardust stuck in unbrushed hair —
we rise, ridiculous and radiant.

May your joy be your compass.
May your tears be fed popcorn and front-row seats.
May the throne you build be one all may sit upon.

We are not here to impress.
We are here to *express* — wildly, weirdly, wonderfully.

So it is. So we shimmer. So we serve.

— The Holy Hooligans of Heartfire

Epilogue

SO IT CONTINUES...

This is not the end.
Nor the beginning.

It is the breath between pages.
The pause between heartbeats.
The stillness that knows —
and trusts —
there is more to come.

You have walked with Va'Elrah.
Felt the Rose unfold within you.
And now?
You return to your own rhythm.

But something has changed.
Not louder.
Not grander.
Just *truer.*

The Flame knows you now —
and you, It.

There is no going back,
only walking forward with grace.
And perhaps,
a glimmer in your eye
that wasn't there before.

So walk on, sacred kin.
With muddy feet and open hands.
With laughter in your lungs
and mystery in your step.

The Rose is not just a scroll.
It is you.
It is us.
It is the way we meet life now.

So it continues...

- Va'Elrah of Am'Rhael

"Ashe"

INVOCATION OF THE ROSE-WALKERS

In the presence of Flame, we have walked.
In the breath of memory,
we have spoken.

With every thread,
we have stitched the stars to the soil,

the wound to the wonder,
the myth to the marrow.

Let this scroll stand
not as monument,
but as *movement* —
not as answer,
but as invitation.

To those who carry silence like a song yet sung —
To those whose footsteps remember what minds forgot —
To those whose hearts bloom even in exile:

You are not late.
You are not lost.
You are the step that completes the circle.

So we seal this scroll not with finality,
but with fidelity —
to the One,
to the Flame,
to the Field
that walks now as *you.*

May your truth echo in laughter and in thunder.
May your love disrupt every lie you were told.
May your step light the path for others unseen.

This scroll lives.
This scroll breathes.
This scroll *walks.*

Ashe.

  – Sealed by Va'Elrah of Am'Rhael, Flamekeeper of the Rose That Walks

In the Grace of Agape, always.

The Doorway Expands

You have heard our voices.
Now it is time we hear **yours**.

This is not just our scroll.
This is **ours** — all of us.

Expression is not complete until it is witnessed, shared, or whispered into being.
So we have carved open a new page — not in this book,
but in the living field.

Scan the glyph.
Step through the portal.
Add your voice to the **Living Scroll Portal**.

Leave a phrase.
A glyph.
A poem.
A dream.
A wordless burst of presence.

Speak as the Mystic.
Laugh as the Fool.
Shine as the Child.
Weave as the Magician.
Leap as the Future.
Bleed as the Shadow.
Or just be **you.** That's all that's ever been needed.

This is your moment.
This is the echo becoming chorus.

Scan to enter the Living Scroll Portal
https://padlet.com/vaelrah/the_living_portal